SCATALOG
A Kid's Field Guide to Animal Poop

HOW TO TRACK A BLACK BEAR

Norman D. Graubart

"BECAUSE EVERYBODY POOPS"

WINDMILL
BOOKS

New York

Published in 2015 by Windmill Books, an Imprint of Rosen Publishing
29 East 21st Street, New York, NY 10010

First Edition

Editor: Katie Kawa
Book Design: Michael J. Flynn

Photo Credits: Cover (black bear), pp. 4, 14 Dennis W. Donohue/Shutterstock.com; cover (poop), p. 16 Bob Gurr/All Canada Photos/Getty Images; back cover, pp. 1, 3–8, 10–14, 16–24 (fur) murengstockphoto/Shutterstock.com; pp. 5, 19 (solid poop) Gerald & Buff Corsi/Visuals Unlimited/ Getty Images; p. 6 (American black bear) Critterbiz/Shutterstock.com; p. 6 (Asiatic black bear) Tigger11th/ Shutterstock.com; p. 7 pavalena/Shutterstock.com; p. 8 Purestock/Getty Images; p. 9 altrendo nature/ Altrendo/Getty Images; p. 10 Scenic Shutterbug/Shutterstock.com; pp. 11, 13, 19, 21 (bear footprints) ntnt/ Shutterstock.com; p. 11 Debbie Steinhausser/Shutterstock.com; p. 12 Seney Natural History Association/ flickr.com/photos/seneynwr/7294431120/CC BY-SA 2.0; p. 13 Wayne Lynch/All Canada Photos/ Getty Images; p. 15 Konrad Wothe/LOOK/Getty Images; p. 18 Dave Bonta/www.flickr.com/ photos/89056025@N00/4932362933/CC BY-SA 2.0; p. 19 (loose poop) Gregory K. Scott/Photo Researchers/Getty Images; p. 20 Dr. John D. Cunningham/Visuals Unlimited/Getty Images; p. 21 Ray Pfortner/ Photolibrary/Getty Images; p. 22 Sorin Colac/Shutterstock.com.

Library of Congress Cataloging-in-Publication Data

Graubart, Norman D., author.
  How to track a black bear / Norman D. Graubart.
      pages cm. — (Scatalog : a kid's field guide to animal poop)
  Includes index.
  ISBN 978-1-4777-5427-6 (pbk.)
  ISBN 978-1-4777-5428-3 (6 pack)
  ISBN 978-1-4777-5426-9 (library binding)
  1. Black bear—Juvenile literature. 2. Animal droppings—Juvenile literature. 3. Animal tracks—Juvenile literature. 4. Tracking and trailing—Juvenile literature. I. Title.
  QL737.C27G734 2015
  599.78'5—dc23
                        2014031045

Manufactured in the United States of America

CPSIA Compliance Information: Batch # CW15WM: For Further Information contact Rosen Publishing, New York, New York at 1-800-237-9932

CONTENTS

A COMMON BEAR

Have you ever seen a black bear? This is the most common kind of bear in North America. People sometimes see black bears while camping in forests. Some people even like to hunt black bears.

Not all black bears have black fur. Some are brown, gray, or even white.

seed

Black bear poop can tell hunters what the bear has been eating. The bear that left this poop behind ate berries with many seeds.

Hunters have different ways of looking for black bears. Looking for animals while hunting is called tracking. One way to track black bears is by looking for their poop. Black bear poop tells hunters about black bears in the area. This book will teach you about these big animals and how to use their poop to track them.

LIFE IN THE FOREST

Black bears can be found in most parts of Canada and small areas of Mexico. In the United States, they mainly live in the Rocky Mountains and the Appalachian Mountains, in the Northeast, and on the West Coast. Black bears also live in parts of Alaska.

Asiatic black bear

American black bear

There are two main kinds of black bears. The American black bear lives in North America. The Asiatic black bear lives in Asia. This book will only talk about the American black bear.

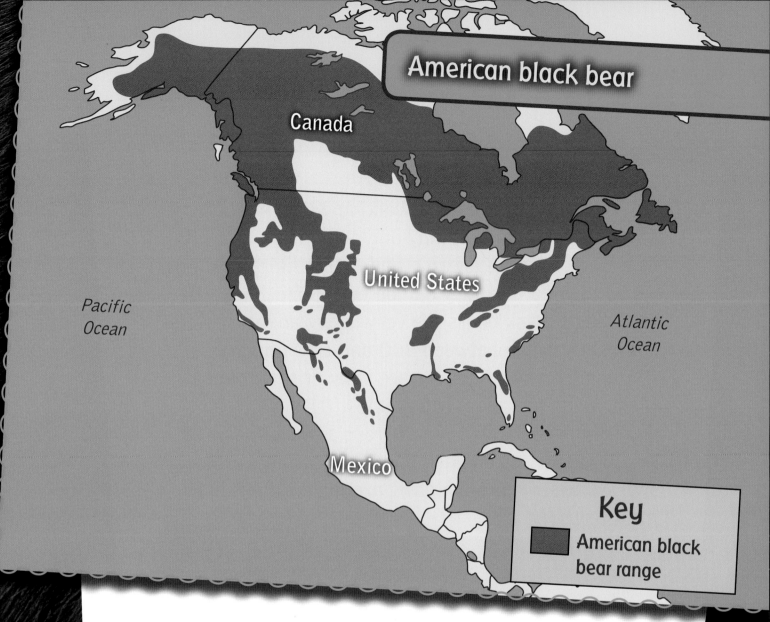

American black bear

Canada

United States

Pacific
Ocean

Atlantic
Ocean

Mexico

Key
American black
bear range

Black bears mostly live in forest **habitats**. These areas have a lot of the trees and other plants that provide food black bears need. Black bears sometimes leave the forest, though. They've been found in southern **swamps** and even in parts of the desert. Sometimes, black bears can wander into neighborhoods where people live as they look for food.

BIG BEARS!

When a black bear is walking with all four paws on the ground, it may only look a few feet tall. However, black bears can stand up on their back legs. When they do this, they can be over 6 feet (1.8 m) tall! Adult black bears are very heavy animals. Males commonly weigh between 200 and 600 pounds (91 and 272 kg). Females are smaller than males. Most weigh less than 200 pounds (91 kg).

Black bears have small front paws with five small, round toes on each paw. They also have short, sharp claws. Their back paws are longer than their front paws.

Black bears use their short claws to help them climb trees.

The black bear is the smallest bear in North America, but it doesn't look very small when it stands on its back legs!

SMART ANIMALS

Black bears are smart animals. They make different noises to **communicate** with each other, as well as with other animals and people. When bears are happy, they make grunting or cooing noises. They can also purr like a cat. When bears are scared, they **huff** and make sharp sounds with their teeth. If hunters hear these noises, they know a bear is in the area.

A group of black bears is sometimes called a sleuth or a sloth.

Most of the time, mothers and babies are the only black bears that stick together.

Black bears are solitary animals. This means they commonly live alone. However, if there's a lot of food in a certain area, they look for food, or forage, together.

Black bears live in an area called a home range. The home range of a female black bear can be as large as 20 square miles (52 sq km). Male home ranges are larger, sometimes reaching over 100 square miles (259 sq km). Often, several female home ranges overlap with a male's home range. This is helpful during **mating** season.

A home range is where a black bear eats, sleeps, mates, and poops. If you find black bear poop on the ground, you've probably walked into a bear's home range.

black bear den

Black bears don't have to eat in the winter because they store up food in their bodies during the warmer months. Black bears aren't true **hibernators**, though. They can wake up from their deep sleep if the weather is warm enough in the winter to forage.

Black bears live in dens during the winter. Their bodies go into a kind of deep sleep called torpor. While they're in this state, they don't eat, drink, or even poop! However, black bears can wake from this state to look for food when the winter weather isn't too cold.

THE LIFE CYCLE OF A BLACK BEAR

Black bears mate during the summer months. Usually, one male will mate with several females. Baby black bears, called cubs, are born in January and February. Usually, mother bears have two to four cubs at a time. Cubs are born blind, and their mother feeds them until spring. Then, they learn to forage. Black bears stay with their mother until they're about two years old.

Black bears can live up to 30 years in the wild. However, most only live to be about 20 years old.

Male black bears play no role in raising cubs.

If you're tracking black bears and see cubs, be careful. Their mother probably isn't too far away, and female black bears are very **protective** of their cubs.

HUNGRY BEARS

Black bears are omnivores. This means they eat both plants and animals. Black bears eat berries, nuts, grasses, roots, bugs, fish, and other animals. Most black bears don't actively hunt, but they do eat dead animals. They also like human food. Black bears will eat food near a campsite or go through trash left by people.

Seeds and pieces of fruits are often seen in black bear poop because they're not easily broken down in a black bear's body. They leave the bear's body with the poop as waste.

BLACK BEAR DIGESTIVE SYSTEM

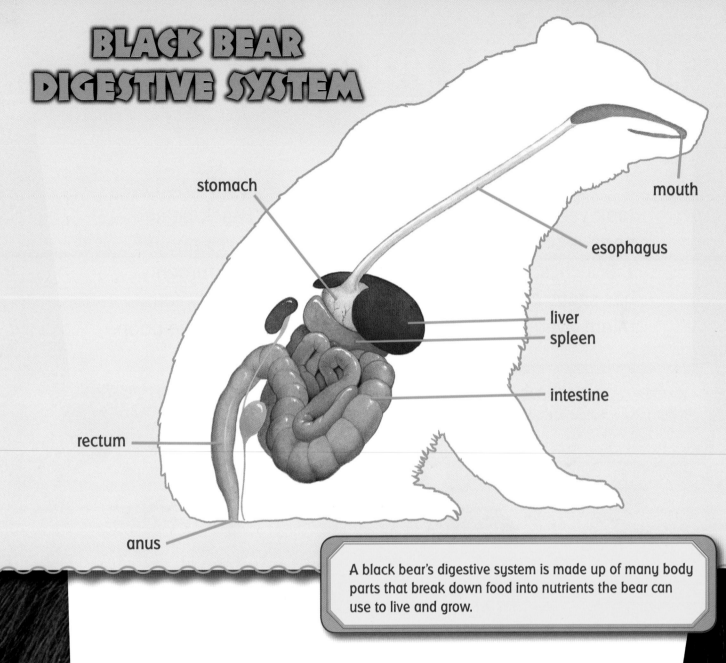

stomach

mouth

esophagus

liver
spleen

intestine

rectum

anus

A black bear's digestive system is made up of many body parts that break down food into nutrients the bear can use to live and grow.

A black bear's digestive system is the group of body parts used to break down its food. The food goes into the stomach. Then, the important **nutrients** are **absorbed** in the intestines to be used by the bear's body.

BLACK BEAR POOP

Because black bears are omnivores, their poop can look very different after different meals. Black bear poop is often shaped like a tube and measures about 1.5 inches (3.8 cm) across. Also, the poop commonly has seeds and other pieces of plant matter in it. You might even find parts of bugs or apple peels in the poop.

A black bear's poop will often smell like the plants it ate. If a bear ate strawberries, its poop would smell like that fruit!

TYPES OF BLACK BEAR POOP

LOOSE

- watery and soft

- comes from eating wet plants or meat

SOLID

- shaped like a tube
- often has plant matter in it

- comes from eating seeds, grasses, and other plants

How can black bear poop help you while hunting? If the poop is shiny or wet, it was probably left recently. This means you're probably in at least one black bear's home range. If you notice blackberry seeds in the poop, look for nearby blackberry bushes. If you find some, the bear might be in the area.

OTHER CLUES

Black bears leave other clues for hunters to follow, too. They use their claws to mark trees. There might be teeth marks in the trees from black bears eating the bark. Bears also rub against trees when they need to scratch, leaving behind their scent as well as other marks for hunters to see.

Black bears mark trees with their claws to show that an area is part of their home range.

4 inches (10 cm)

7 inches (18 cm)

five toes

This track was left by the back foot of a black bear. The front feet leave shorter tracks. Although black bears have claws, you can't always see claw marks on the ground.

Black bear footprints, or tracks, can point you in the direction a bear was traveling. Black bears' tracks look like human footprints, but they're wider and shorter.

Black bears can also be tracked by looking for their den. Areas near the bases of trees are good places to look for dens.

DIFFERENT KINDS OF TRACKERS

Black bears used to live throughout most of North America. Now, they've moved far into forests and mountain areas because of hunting and because they don't like to be around people. **Conservationists** have worked to keep areas safe for black bears. This includes keeping rivers clean, so the salmon these bears eat can live in rivers near black bear populations.

Hunters help keep black bear populations from getting too large. Scientists also track black bears to learn more about them. Both groups of people know the importance of black bear poop!

GLOSSARY

absorb (uhb-ZOHRB) To take in or soak up.

communicate (kuh-MYOO-nuh-kayt) To share ideas or feelings.

conservationist (kahn-suhr-VAY-shuh-nihst) A person who wants to keep natural resources safe.

habitat (HAA-buh-tat) The natural home for plants, animals, and other living things.

hibernator (HY-buhr-nay-tuhr) An animal whose body shuts down during the winter months and can't be woken.

huff (HUHF) To puff, or breathe hard.

mate (MAYT) To come together to make babies.

nutrient (NOO-tree-uhnt) Something taken in by a plant or animal that helps it grow and stay healthy.

protective (pruh-TEHK-tihv) Wanting to keep something safe.

swamp (SWAHMP) Soft, wet land often partly covered with water.

INDEX

WEBSITES

For web resources related to the subject of this book, go to:
www.windmillbooks.com/weblinks and select this book's title.